make your own

Quilting Designs & Patterns

Judy Woodworth

American Quilter's Society
P. O. Box 3290 • Paducah, KY 42002-3290
www.AmericanQuilter.com

Located in Paducah, Kentucky, the American Quilter's Society (AQS) is dedicated to promoting the accomplishments of today's quilters. Through its publications and events, AQS strives to honor today's quiltmakers and their work and to inspire future creativity and innovation in quiltmaking.

Executive Editor: Andi Milam Reynolds
Senior Editor: Linda Baxter Lasco
Graphic Design: Lynda Smith
Copy Editor: Elaine Brelsford
Cover Design: Michael Buckingham
Photography: Charles R. Lynch
How-to Photography: Judy Woodworth

Additional copies of this book may be ordered from the American Quilter's Society, PO Box 3290, Paducah, KY 42002-3290, or online at www.AmericanQuilter.com.

Text ©2012, Author, Judy Woodworth
Artwork ©2012, American Quilter's Society

Library of Congress Cataloging-in-Publication Data

Woodworth, Judy.
  Make your own quilting designs and patterns / by Judy Woodworth.
    pages cm
  ISBN 978-1-60460-035-3
  1. Quilting--Patterns. 2. Quilts--Design. I. Title.
  TT835.W6597 2012
  746.46--dc23
                          2012025007

Dedication

When my husband, Woody, insisted that I submit another book proposal to the American Quilter's Society on how I develop my quilting ideas, I don't think he realized all the work he was setting himself up for in the process.

He has always been a great cook, but he really stepped up and helped me with laundry and cleaning. Can you imagine that? He has a full-time banking job but that didn't stop him from doing any chore I needed help with including shopping and doing all the driving on long trips so I could type away at my computer in the car.

He believes in me and constantly encourages me to achieve my professional dreams. Isn't he a great guy? I'm so lucky and I dedicate this book to him.

"Honey, I promise, after this book is written that I'll clear the dining room table and serve you a meal at the table."

Also, I would like to give a big Thank You to my best friend Mary Sue Suit for allowing me to quilt her beautiful pieced quilts. You'll see how I designed the quilting patterns for a few of her amazing quilts starting on page 28.

Thanks to Jessica Schick from Digi-Tech for digitizing many of the patterns in this book. And thanks to my friend Sherry Rogers Harrison for her interpretation of my Feathers and Pearls pattern. Her AUTUMN BUTTERNUT quilt is on page 69.

Pat Bell

Contents

HERE KITTY, KITTY, detail,
full quilt on page 75

Introduction

Many of you know me from my first book, *Freemotion Quilting*, and know how much I love quilting designs without marking my quilt. What you may not know is that several times a year, I do totally mark my quilts when I create original patterns and quilts. To be a complete quilter and designer, you need to be able to add both to your overall quilting skills.

I will show you several different methods to design quilting patterns and how to design wholecloth quilts either from ready-made stencils or your own quilting patterns. You'll learn how to draw quilts in miniature, enlarge the pattern, and draw full-size designs.

There are many pieced or appliquéd quilts that require very special symmetrical quilting patterns that you can design. But when you look at those big white spaces where you will be designing a pattern, it seems almost overwhelming. How do you even start? I'll try to show you how I do it.

I'll even throw in information about how to design and quilt thread-painted quilts and on quilting designs that can be painted. There is also a chapter on how to draft a Mariner's Compass or Mariner's Star that can be just quilted as a wholecloth quilt, or painted, or pieced.

For those who just want to use my patterns, I've included many to get you started. I'll show how some of them look using matching thread, contrasting thread, variegated thread, or even painted.

This book is not your typical "here are some patterns you can transfer to your quilt" book. I truly believe that every one of you has the ability to do some unique designing of your own.

Now don't throw down the book and run out the door screaming. You can do this! And they'll be your original designs. I'll be there helping you all along this journey.

Get your pencil sharpened. Here we go.

Inspiration

You don't need to be told to keep your eyes open, because if you are a quilter, you already look at everything to see if there is a quilting pattern or a quilt in what you see.

This metal fruit basket stopped me short in a buffet line and off I went to get my digital camera. We were in Paducah and other quilters knew exactly what I was doing…great structure for a quilting pattern.

This is where I tell you that you absolutely cannot copy someone else's art work without their permission, but you can be inspired and motivated by it. Take a curved line or a leaf out of their design and see where it will take you. The fruit basket did become the inspiration for a quilting design (page 51).

Books from Dover Publications are another source where you can get zillions of copyright-free designs for your own personal use. My recommendation is not to copy them completely but to add your own touches to their designs.

Flowers can be a great starting point for a design and you can photograph flowers right in your own garden. No one is going to come knocking on your door and hand you a lawsuit document for infringing on copyright laws. It's time to come up with your own ideas.

You have my permission to make a quilt in your interpretation of my photos.

See how you can take this sunflower photo and make it into your own pattern.

I can enlarge my quilting pattern and use all the small details as shown in this drawing. If I were to quilt the size shown, I might need to remove some of the small details and simplify the design. I actually digitized this pattern in my BERNINA software program so that I could embroider it.

This sunflower was also the inspiration for a very different quilting design in my quilt that was a finalist in the Sunflower: New Quilts from an Old Favorite contest sponsored by The National Quilt Museum.

GRAFFITI, SUNFLOWERS & BRICKS, detail

GRAFFITI, SUNFLOWERS & BRICKS, 71" x 71", designed and quilted by the author, painted by Bill Woodworth

There are many books that are filled with patterns and patterns for you to copy, and you can even get other patterns by the hundreds in such programs as The Electric Quilt Company or from people who digitize patterns (see Resources, page 78). I'm hoping that I can convince you to break out and design your own patterns and quilts.

You need to condition your husband (or wife) that when you screech on your brakes to take a picture of a design on the outside of someone's house, he (or she) should not panic or call 911. My husband is well-conditioned and either laughs at me or sinks down in his seat so no one can see him.

Most of my feather designs are built off stems or spirals. Therefore I am always on the lookout for spirals. Sometimes I find them in wall decorations or on a rusty old iron gate. My camera is always with me. It's important to look for interesting shapes that can inspire you to design a feather motif.

I loved the way the spirals in this ironwork piece seemed to caress each other and I just knew there had to be a quilting pattern in there.

Rough draft drawn of half the design inspired by the gate

Pattern simplified and digitized by Jessica Schick of Digi-Tech, detailed version on page 62

Look at some of the photos I have taken and see if any of them inspire you to a new design idea. Remember, no copying.

The veins of a leaf can give you a starting point for a quilting pattern.

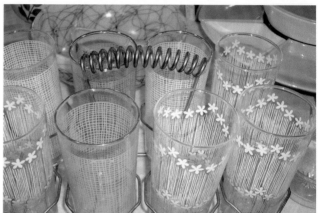

The curly spiral in the glass holder can be incorporated into any number of designs.

The curves of the violin bases in my son's band room, where he is the director, instantly inspired an idea for a quilt design. Wouldn't it be fun to do fusible appliqué in bright colors?

The picture of these boats at a lake near Paducah will surely inspire you. You have my permission to take this picture to develop a quilt composition.

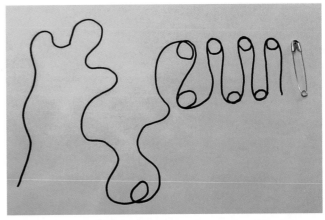

Remember, your inspiration can be as small as a safety pin. It is just a line that swirls and curls into a safety pin quilting design that can be used in a border.

These fish are in a fish tank in Vegas. Nature just gets it right. Notice the big and the little lines and dots that create such unity.

Even the fins on my grandson's fish could be the beginning of a good design (see page 65). And don't you just love Ryan's smile? I see a pictorial quilt in my future.

Flowers are both graceful and exotic. Try to create the two conflicting emotions in one quilting design.

Sometimes a free-motion design is the perfect candidate for a fun curly quilting pattern, so take photos of every design you do.

Tumbling Rainbow, detail, full quilt on page 70

Even a single musical instrument can be the inspiration for an entire quilt.

Harp in Minor, 17" x 17", made by the author, photo by Marilyn Karper

Preparing to Create

Before I begin any project, I lie down on my bed in a quiet room. I do some Lamaze breathing exercises to help me totally relax. (Having five kids naturally had long-term benefits.)

Take three deep cleansing breaths and as you breathe in, say quietly in your mind, "Relax, relax, relax." As you slowly expel your breath, visualize all the tension leaving your body. Concentrate on relaxing each and every muscle until you feel like you are floating.

Then it begins. Think about the project you are starting and let your creative mind explore many possibilities. You are not going to sleep, unless you really need to, but you are going to visualize how a certain project or problem with your design can be embellished or revised. I have come up with so many good ideas this way.

Get up and quickly draw or write down your ideas. The seed is planted. Let it grow.

If you get nothing, try a different tactic. Take a leisurely walk or go to a museum or an art store and let their creativity fill your soul. Again, not copying anything—just opening up to the possibilities.

During the loading of a quilt on my longarm, I concentrate deeply on the feel of the fabric, the patterns in the fabric, and the piecing or appliqué design, shutting out the rest of the world. Usually, a few things start popping into my mind. It's scary quilting someone else's masterpiece. Being scared usually puts the brakes on creativity, although sometimes it starts your adrenalin flowing, which might not be a bad thing.

I begin quilting by sewing the first border ditch line, focusing on getting my mind and body into a relaxed state. Once I have sewn that line, there is no turning back, no room for fear or failure. Try it. Suddenly, your mind starts adding on to the original thoughts of design you have and things fall into place.

The same is true for designing a quilting pattern. Put down your initial spirals and then start experimenting with pencil. (Erasers are so great. Kudos to whoever invented them.)

Eliminating Fear

Don't give up before you even begin. You can learn to draw feathers and designs. I will show you how (pages 18–24).

For those of you absolutely terrified of drawing, there are two books I recommend: *Drawing on the Right Side of the Brain* by Betty Edwards and *Drawing the Light from Within: Keys to Awaken Your Creative Power* by Judith Cornell.

Both books talk about using the creative side of your brain or soul. We all have to find the key that opens up the sometimes hidden treasure stored deep within our soul. Betty's book gives you several exercises that open up the right (creative) side of your brain and keeps the left (critical thinking) side of the brain busy somewhere else.

Judith tries to help you dive deep into your soul and fill it with love and creativity by having you do relaxation techniques by visualizing what she calls "The Hall of Illumined Arts and Design." You visualize the story she tells you that will help you get to the hall where creativity and art is created.

To sum up—what both of them try to do is to get you in a special place, mentally and emotionally, where you can deeply focus on creating without fear. Fear and lack of confidence is what holds many people back from achieving the freedom to create original designs and quilts. Trust me on this: when you start designing your own patterns and quilts, your self-confidence will soar to new levels you never thought you could achieve. I promise it will make you happy.

Sounds too easy, right? But nothing is better than being happy and complete no matter how bad things might be everywhere around you. And it's a lot cheaper than therapy.

The easiest way I have found to inspire creativity is to surround myself and my spirit with beautiful objects. They don't have to be expensive, even garage sale items can be inspiring. Look at a tea cup with graceful flowers, or a vase with wonderful swirls, or flowers in your garden, and you'll start the process of awakening a sleeping lioness.

Let your personality show through and you'll grow strong as an artist.

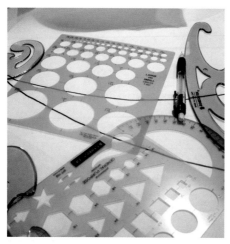

Getting Started

I'm sure you have heard that if you don't have the proper supplies and tools, your job will be so much harder. Designing patterns and quilts is no exception. These tools will make your designing more professional. Most of these tools can be purchased in the engineering department of an office supply store. Circle templates, some with triangles, stars, Mars French curves will all help when you are ready to perfect your drawing—that is, to smooth out the lines of a free-hand drawn pattern (see Resources, page 78).

Supplies

Circle templates

Quilter's Design Mirrors

Mars French curves

Black Sharpie® permanent marker

Mechanical pencils or lead pencils

Automatic pencil sharpener

Flex curves in several sizes

Half-square triangle template

Sketch pads and books

20-weight copier paper

Freezer paper

Infinite Feathers templates by Anita Shackelford

Compass

Protractor

Sharp-edge straight-line rulers

Travel artist's workstation

Quality white eraser (essential!)

Water-soluble blue pens

White mechanical chalk pens

Various rotary cutter rulers

Computer and scanner/printer (or copy shop that will enlarge your patterns)

Light box

Inspirational items

Computer software that will let you "tile print" the design in the enlarged size (optional)

How to Begin

I usually draw my design freehand, never stopping to perfect the drawing until I am finished. I do not want anything to interrupt my creativity. (More details about this in the next chapter.) Sometimes I draw the design in miniature and perfect it with the smallest of the circle templates. Other times, I will enlarge the design to the full size of the quilt and then make all the super-fine adjustments, perfecting it at the larger size.

You will definitely need double-sided Quilter's Design Mirrors created by Jan Krentz. The two hinged panels are an extra large 8½" x 11". They are ideal for seeing how your design is progressing when you only draw one-half, one-quarter, or even one-eighth of the design. The satisfaction of seeing how the complete design will look showing in mirror image will really get you excited.

Viewing half a design with the Quilter's Design Mirrors

When you travel or watch TV, you need a portable workstation that will keep your supplies and paper at your fingertips. Doodling alone will sometimes lead to a design. If you have an iPad you can download either of these two great apps for doodling (Penultimate or Whiteboard) and save all your drawings in one spot.

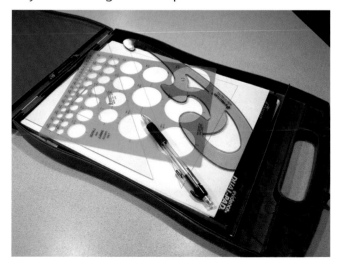

At the very least, always have a sketchbook with you for doodling ideas.

Flex curves come in various sizes. I have one that lies flat and it is just right when I want to draw pearls (circles) within a curve. The skinnier one is the right size for stems where feathers can grow.

Don't forget those inspirational items. I loved the photo of these flowers and modified it for this floral design.

There is always a reason to go to antique stores and I have an obsession for antique pins. I wear them, but mostly, I am inspired by them. This pin became the inspiration for a stained-glass quilt (page 47) and for a thread-painted quilt (page 71).

My computer and scanner/printer are as important in my sewing room as my sewing machine. Since I live in a rural town in Nebraska, I have to rely on myself at home to enlarge my patterns. My two favorite software programs are CorelDRAW® and Adobe® Photoshop®. Before I got the full version of Photoshop, I had the Photoshop Elements, which is much less expensive but does the job. I can draw one-eighth of my design and scan it into my computer. I mirror image it and print out four of the original drawings and four mirror-image copies that I can quickly put together with tape, forming a complete design.

Another option is to tape one original and one mirror image together, scan them, save them, and "import" the image into CorelDRAW. I duplicate my drawing and mirror image, put them side-by-side, and group them as one drawing. Then I select the custom size and enter ¼ the size of the full quilt, for example 36" by 36". I can resize the drawing by stretching it to 36". Then I can go to the print page, select "tile", and it will print out the individual pages of the drawing. I will tape each page together with regular tape, making sure it is straight and fits like a puzzle.

I double-check with a square ruler that it is straight, turn it over, tape the joins with strong shipping tape, and this becomes my master pattern. I can copy it four times on the fabric to make a complete design.

If you have a copy center that can enlarge your design, you can go have your line drawings enlarged. Some copy centers only go up to 36" in width and as long as you want, but some go up to 45" wide. The paper comes on a roll and it's great for making a master pattern.

The Harp Quilt

I have always loved harps and the quilting design for this wholecloth quilt top was inspired by the harp. I first did a one-eighth drawing.

I reviewed it with the double-sided mirror so I could see how the entire design would look on the quilt before I used my computer to mirror and duplicate it into a full-size drawing.

This is the rough computer design. I didn't do the final perfecting until I enlarged the pattern.

Harp detail, full quilt on page 73, miniature version of this quilt in the Inspiration section, page 10

Designing a Quilt Top

The same technique for creating quilting designs can be used to design a quilt top. In my design classes, I will draw one of my original designs on the whiteboard, similar to a Ricky Tims' Rhapsody quilt design. The class has to follow me to draw the gentle curve in the same approximate place on their 8½" x 11" paper.

I am always surprised that so many students who think they can't draw do a pretty darn good job of placing the lines in the right places. Then I take the two-sided mirror around and they are amazed at the design they have drawn—slightly different from mine, but still beautiful.

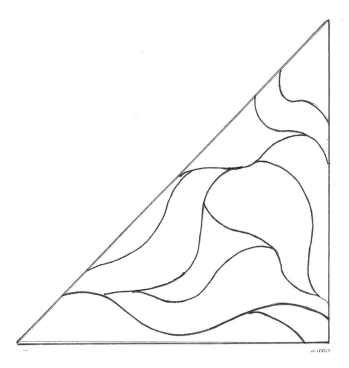

At this point you could mark a square on a 36" by 36" piece of freezer paper, made by taping or gluing narrow sheets together. Draw a diagonal line corner to corner. Take your small drawing and, looking back and forth between it and the full-size freezer paper, transfer your lines in their approximate place on the larger paper. It may be slightly different but it will be pretty close to your original drawing. Now fold the freezer paper in half on the diagonal line and transfer the lines to the other side to form a one-fourth master pattern.

Or you can take your small, one-fourth design you have created to a copy center and enlarge it to 36" by 36" inches, which is one-fourth of your full-size pattern.

Here the one-eighth drawing has been mirror-imaged in Photoshop, printed, then taped together to form one-fourth of the quilt design. It was then scanned again into Photoshop and saved before it was "imported" into the CorelDRAW program. From there, I made a duplicate and mirrored it vertically. I "group" these two drawings, make a duplicate of the now half of the quilt, then I mirror it horizontally, and join them together to make my full Tulip quilt.

Once you enlarge your pattern, get out the fabric you think would look good in the quilt. Lay your fabric on the pattern so you can study where the colors and values should go in your quilt.

Designing a Quilting Pattern

After you find the inspiration for your design, you need to be able to draw feathers, fleur-de-lis, flowers, spirals, or even dinosaurs—whatever design your quilt needs. Sometimes you'll just be designing one pattern that will fit in all the blocks. If you have a longarm machine, you could even use your laser to follow the lines of your pattern while you machine quilt the design. If you have a computerized machine, you can digitize the patterns to quilt your blocks.

In most cases you will have to transfer the design onto your quilt top by placing the design under your quilt, using a light box if necessary, and marking with a blue water-soluble marker, a chalk pencil or a purple air-disappearing marker. Note that the air-disappearing marks go away quickly. You would need to quilt that design within one hour to one day, depending on the humidity in your area. The higher the humidity, the faster the purple marks will disappear.

Feathers

Let's get back to the drawing of the pattern. I'll start with feathers. There are so many different types of feathers. Here are some of the feathers that I use. Notice that they are all unique. You must match the personality of the feather to the personality of the quilt—formal to formal, funky to funky, and so on.

On the informal feather, there is a slight gap between each feather. If the heart was drawn, it would be along the stem line on the other side.

When you are learning to draw feathers, it's a good idea to draw an outside line with a fine pencil where the edge of the feather should stop, so that you have a little uniformity in the size of the feathers. (Honestly though, most of my feathers often have different sizes and shapes.)

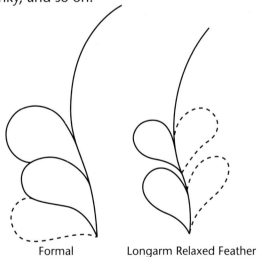

Formal   Longarm Relaxed Feather

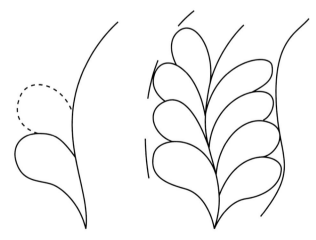

The formal feather has each feather intersect at about the midpoint of the bump of the previous feather. You can almost visualize that if you completed the heart shape, it would fall on the outside edge, where the dots are.

After I draw my stem line using a curved flex ruler to get the shape I want, I draw my first feather normally. For all the rest of the feathers, I start at the mid bump of the feather and smoothly draw a round top, then down to the stem line. A forty-five degree angle is about normal, but don't limit your feathers to being this exact.

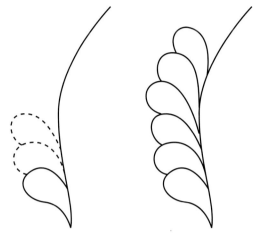

Drawing formal feathers

The rounded edges of this informal feather resembles plants found in nature.

Drawing informal feathers

For an even more natural look, give each feather a dimple and vein line instead of rounding the ends.

Okay, those of you who are now feeling a little panicky, take a breath. There is a wonderful template out there called Infinite Feathers by Anita Shackelford (see Resources, page 78). Select the feather shape you want and draw each gracefully on your stem line at an approximate 45-degree angle.

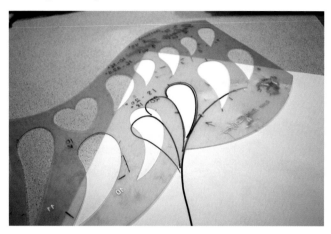

Using her template ensures all your feathers will be the same size. See? You can do this. Now relax.

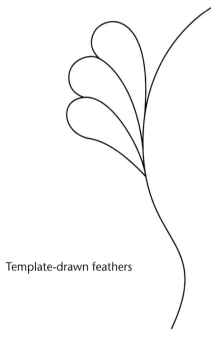

Template-drawn feathers

Another method is to draw your stem using the flex curve ruler, then use a circle template to draw half circles beyond the stem. Butt each half circle against the previous one. Draw an outline where the top of the circles should line up, or place them at varying heights.

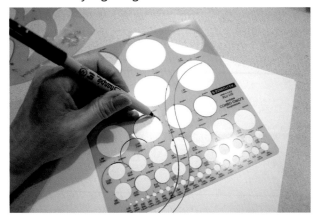

It looks funny now, but look at those perfectly rounded tops that will become feathers. You are starting with perfect tops to your feathers.

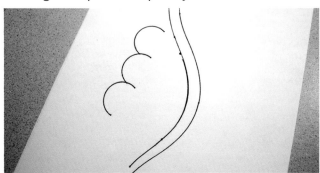

I usually freely draw my feathers first, then perfect them by putting the circle template on top of the roughly drawn feathers and smoothing out the lines. Try both ways and see which works for you.

Pick a Mars French curve with the right shape and finish each feather smoothly and gracefully to the stem.

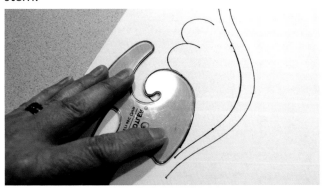

Feel free to mark circles within the stems.

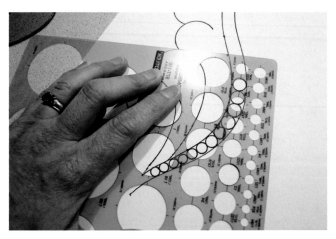

Get your circle template out and try to finish this feather.

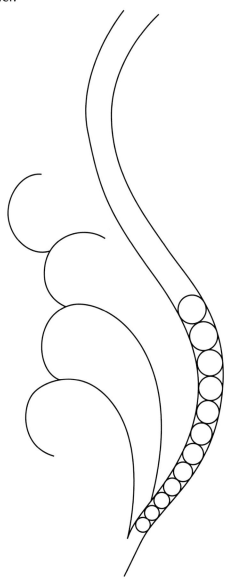

Other Feather Styles and Techniques

Try some stacked feathers, made famous by Irena Bluhm. Start with a teardrop in the middle and stack your feathers on top of the teardrop.

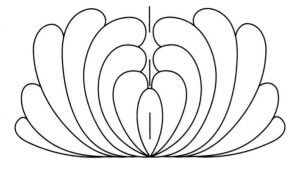

Stacked feathers

Draw one-half of a design, fold the paper in half, and use your light box to complete the other half of the design.

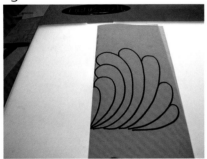

There are many areas in a pieced quilt where patches come to a point, like in a Lone Star quilt. Use a compass to draw a circular line touching the tips of the Lone Star piecing. Then draw a second circular line. One is for the outside edge of your feathers and one is for where the feathers intersect on the middle of the bump.

I call the resulting design a fan feather, which adds interest to a pieced point having soft feathers at the tip.

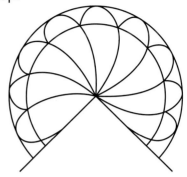

Fan feathers

If you want to perfect it first, use your compass to draw the two semicircles. Draw the tops of your feathers with a circle template. With a long Mars French curve, draw lines to the center. You could divide the feathers using a protractor to get perfect divisions, or fold in half, fold again, and again until you get the size you want for your feathers and pick a circle template that fits this division.

You could mirror image fan feathers with a teardrop in the middle. Do half the feathers, fold in half at the teardrop, and use a light box to draw a symmetrical mirror image.

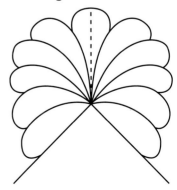

Mirror-image fan feathers

Create kissing feathers that are divided by a line in the middle of the concave parts of a curved stem. Draw feathers up to the line, reducing the size of the feathers until you are at the stem. Then draw the next feather doing a backbend to touch and kiss the feathers you just drew.

Backbend feathers

You can stop anytime to perfect the tips of each feather with a circle template. Just don't let it stop your creativity!

Perfecting the feather tips

A comma-shaped design has a small circle at the tip. Use it in your feather design to break up the feathers and give them personality. One of

these comma feathers has even been made into a pregnant comma feather. It can curl clear around in a circle before you put the little circle tip and start following it back to the stem. One of the feathers below also has a curl inside the feather, an element often found in antique quilts.

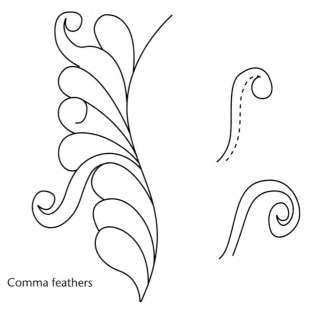

Comma feathers

Curly feathers are wonderful for certain types of quilts. Don't forget to do some backbend feathers as a surprise. And don't forget to perfect the tips of the feathers when you are through drawing them freehand.

Curly feathers

Disappearing feathers look like they have been tucked under another feather. Draw dashed lines where the feather would go under the other feather, so you can visualize where the hidden feather is.

Disappearing feathers

Long and skinny feathers can look like they are opening up and lying out backwards. These feathers need to be quilted with the bump-back technique, where you have a long, single line on the feather with the backtracking done at the top of the feather.

Pencil Transfer Design

When you draw the center of a four-sided design, you can transfer the design without a light box by using a heavy lead pencil and inexpensive paper (20 weight) that you can see through. Fold the drawing with the lead pencil markings to the INSIDE so that the drawing touches the area where you want to transfer the design. On the back side of that folded paper, you will be able to faintly see the lead pencil drawing. Draw heavily on the faint line. When you open up the paper, the lead pencil will have transferred lightly to the other side. Now you can outline both design areas with a Sharpie permanent marker.

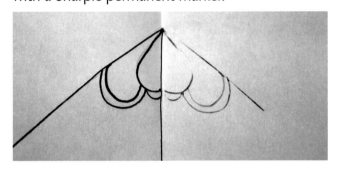

Use your double-sided mirror to see if you like the design.

Checking the design with a mirror

Repeat these steps to trace and transfer the other half of the design so the design is complete.

Design Example

I found inspiration for a design with this metal decoration that is on my front room wall.

I drew half of my design and used the pencil transfer method as described above.

Here's the complete design. Enjoy using this on a quilt of your own.

Designing a Full Quilt

When I am designing a quilt, whether a wholecloth or one that I am going to piece or appliqué, I usually start by drawing a half-square triangle.

There are several ways to draw a perfect half-square triangle. Use a square ruler and a fine mechanical pencil to mark a 7½" by 7½" square, then draw a line from corner to corner.

On a computer, go to Accessories and select Paint. In Paint, select the rectangle and as you drag it, hold down the shift key to make a perfect square. Select the line draw tool and divide the square in half diagonally. You will only be drawing on one-half of the square.

In a drawing program, you can drag a square tool, usually holding down the Ctrl key, and it will give you a perfect square. Select the top left corner "node" and delete. The line will straighten out, giving you a perfect half-square triangle.

I know I've gone on about this, but if you don't start with a perfectly marked half-square triangle, when you mirror image the other half and connect the two halves, you will not have a perfect square. If you don't have a perfect square, you will never have a straight quilt.

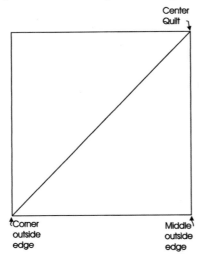

Your half-square triangle is where you will draw your design in miniature. I like to start in the center of the quilt and work out. Some people do better designing from the outside in. Some design best by block or row. Everyone is wired differently. Once you start experimenting, you will discover which method works best for you.

Keep in mind that your quilt, depending on how big it is going to be, needs three or four divisions, including the border. They must look proportionally pleasing to the eye. There may be some scientific rules, as determined by the Romans or someone, but I am telling you to start trusting your gut. The center of a mirror-image, symmetrical quilt should be the main focus, and everything else should complement it and draw your eye to the center of the quilt. After you design a quilt, look for problem areas.

In this example, arrows show areas needing correction.

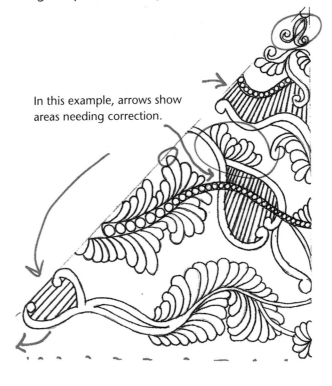

For my most recent wholecloth quilt, I identified the areas that I needed to correct before I enlarged the pattern. I needed to add another element on the bottom or move the bottom harp lower to be in a straight line with the other element. The mid-area that is circled needs to be redrawn and mirror imaged (see page 25).

When the now-corrected one-eighth drawing was enlarged, I put freezer paper over it. When I was ready to trace the design, I took my circle template and corrected the top of each feather. I drew all the harp's radiating lines using Renae Haddadin's Amazing Rays tools (see Resources, page 78). I also could have used a protractor and larger ruler.

Another design method is to do a collage of copyright-free drawings. I took photos and cut out these cat pictures. I enlarged or reduced some of them until they were pleasingly the right size to arrange on 8½" x 11" paper. I only wanted the drawings, not so that I could copy them, but because I wanted a realistic outline drawing of the cats. I outlined the cats on another piece of paper, using a light box.

Then I enlarged my drawing to the actual size of the quilt. I transferred the outlines of the cats to a 100 percent cotton piece of muslin with pencil. I hung the muslin on my design wall and drew what I imagined was the insides of the cats where I would be adding appliqué. Occasionally, I would look back at my original collage to see if I was placing the eyes and mouths in the approximate place. My design within the outlines was totally original.

By drawing in an upright position, you can stand back and see how your quilt will look after the design is completed.

I took my colored pencils and sketched approximately where I would place certain colors—all subject to change at any time—on my original 8½" x 11" copy.

I cut out bits of colorful fabrics and started placing them on the cats, changing my mind at any time to get the effect I wanted. Since I was not piecing, I could change things around with more serendipity than if I needed to be exact for piecing.

I can just barely see my pencil marks on the fabric, giving me an approximate place to build my cats.

Here is the finished quilt.

Here Kitty, Kitty, 77" x 52½", made by the author, see the Gallery, page 75

I created Avatar Revisited with the same technique by drawing one-eighth of my design.

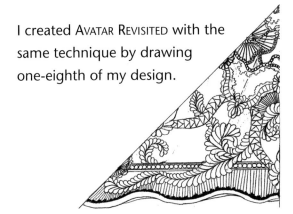

In the computer I duplicated and mirror imaged the one-eighth design. After putting all the sections together, I used my colored pencils, not so much for the exact color that I would use, but to indicate areas of light, medium, and dark. I

wanted to see if this could be done with colored thread in a wholecloth.

Avatar Revisited, back detail

I was able to enlarge just one-fourth of the pattern and transfer it to the black sateen fabric by using a light box. The black cotton sateen had been subdivided into quarters with registration lines. I used both Fons & Porter's mechanical chalk pencil and a Bohin mechanical chalk pencil. Previously I had tested this chalk to make sure it would not rub off during the quilting and that it could be removed with a damp microfiber cloth.

Avatar Revisited, made by the author, from the main collection of The National Quilt Museum

So you see, you can do a white or black wholecloth using this pattern-enlarging method. You can also make a pieced or appliquéd quilt using this same technique as I did for my quilt The Fragile World (page 33).

Designing for a Pieced Top

My quilt is pieced. Now what do I do?

Everyone, if given the chance, might decide to quilt the same pieced quilt very differently. There are no right or wrong decisions about this. It's very personal. It is not a difficult process if you take one step at a time.

Measure the area to be quilted.
Lay freezer paper cut to that size over the quilt.
Use a water-soluble marker to trace the shape of the area to be quilted.

Remove the paper and trace over the water-soluble lines with a permanent marker.
Fold the paper in half (quarters, or eighths) and draw a half (quarter, or eighth) of your quilting design.
Use a mirror to see how the full design will look.
Perfect the design, using tools to smooth out the lines.
Transfer the design to the remaining section(s) of the paper.
Place the final design under the quilt top and mark the design on the quilt top.

Kiss of Spring, 80" x 80", original design by Mary Sue Suit, quilted by the author, see the Gallery, page 74

Designing for a Quilt

This is how I designed the quilting pattern for my friend Mary Sue Suit's pieced quilt top. I had lots of fun designing this quilt and both Mary Sue and I are very pleased with how it came out. And that's what is important—being satisfied with the work you complete.

The first thing to do is measure the area you're designing and cut freezer paper that size. Sometimes you will have to use two pieces of freezer paper because the area is so large.

Just a tiny little area of freezer paper needs to overlap. If you are making a design for appliqué, use freezer-paper tape, which can stand the heat of the iron. On a quilting pattern, you might need a light box to be able to see the pattern. If you plan to iron the pattern to the back of your pieced top prior to using a light box, either glue pieces of freezer paper together with Roxanne's Glue Baste-it or freezer-paper tape. If you plan to pin the pattern under the pieced top, you can just use clear tape.

Lay the freezer paper over the quilt top and use a blue water-soluble marker to trace over the areas where you want to put a pattern. You want to use a water-soluble marker because you do not want to accidently break through the freezer paper with pencil, pen, or black marker, and ruin the quilt.

You can easily see through the freezer paper, but use a light box if you have any trouble seeing the quilt top.

Remove the freezer paper from the quilt and move the quilt to a safe location. Go over the blue water soluble lines with a black Sharpie.

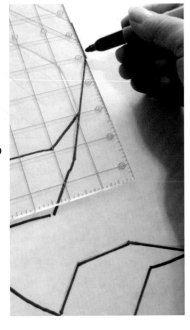

Hang the quilt on your design wall so you can look at it as you decide what kind of design you want to draw. You can also pin a sheet to a quilt rack and pin the quilt to the sheet so you can view it upright, or maybe even pin it to a long curtain.

If the quilt is symmetrical, as it is in this case, you want to keep the quilting pattern symmetrical, too. Fold the paper in half and draw just half the design in pencil. It's scary to see all that blank space. But if you just start in one spot and work on it, generally the rest of the design will come to you.

With half the design done, get out a mirror tool to see if you like how it looks. Make any changes you like.

After you're satisfied with how the design looks, staple the paper to the folded edge so that it will not move during the drawing process. When you turn it over to draw the other side in mirror image it will stay in place. You want both halves of your patterns to be exactly alike.

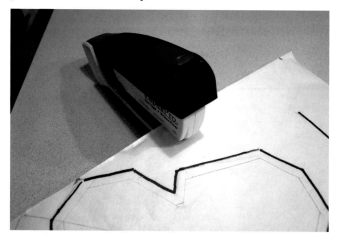

Once you're happy with the design, use the drawing tools (page 12) to smooth out the lines and perfect your design. A flexible ruler is ideal for stems.

Use a professional combo circle template (found at office supply stores in the engineering/drafting department) to make perfect circles. Drawing feathers freehand first allows you to be very creative. Then go back with the circle template to make sure the top of each feather has a nice round shape. Judges will always comment if you don't have a nice, smooth round shape at the top of your feathers.

I like to do more advanced feathers where they fold under other feathers. I either project with my mind where the feather would go under the other feather, or I will just use tiny little dashes to remind me what the feather would look like underneath, so that I come out in the correct spot under the feather.

This was a center design. I am glad I used the two-sided mirror to look at it before I drew it in all eight sections. I didn't like the design I had drawn. I felt I should keep with similar feathers as in the rest of the design.

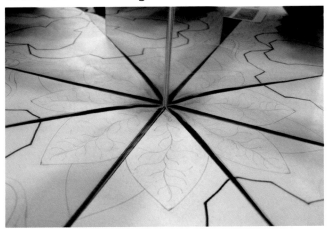

Use various curve templates to help you get a smooth line.

I was considering doing some radiating lines in the white area in middle of the flowers, so I marked some division lines.

Pin your partial design over the quilt and stand back to look at it. Now is the time to decide if the design is flowing or if you need to make changes. You must "listen to your quilt" and it will tell you what you need to do. Don't be afraid to change your design. This is how I discovered that instead of radiating lines, I wanted Strings of Pearls to undulate through each section all around the quilt.

The quilting design should complement the quilt and be in perfect harmony with the pieced design. They should be equal partners, not one more important than the other, unless you really mean for the quilting to be the star.

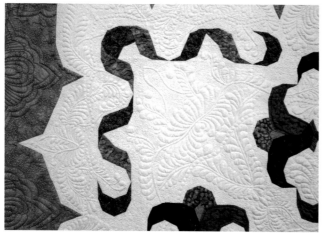

Kiss of Spring, 80" x 80", detail, see the Gallery, page 74

When your quilting design is complete, in the case of symmetrical designs, you can turn over the design you drew on freezer paper and iron it to the back of your pieced top. It will still match up in reverse. On an asymmetrical design, you'll need to pin the freezer paper, right-side up, to the back of the quilt top.

With some white fabrics you don't even need to use a light box. It's rare that the fabric is so thick you can't see through it but it does happen. On Victorian Lace, Mary Sue used a fabric called Fairy Frost. It was a little heavier material and I was not able to see through it without a light box. There were a few spots where I could not see through where two seams were sewn together.

If this happens, just draw what you can see before and after the seam. When you finish marking your top and remove the pattern from the back, lay it on top of the quilt, then free draw the lines you couldn't see through the seam.

If you aren't happy with your drawings, just keep redesigning. If it still doesn't work, get away from it for a while and start over later.

If what you did makes you smile, go with it. If you keep tinkering with it you may never get it finished. Trust yourself and move on to marking the quilt.

Now pull up a chair, get out your blue water-soluble marker (or other marking tool) and begin tracing the pattern onto your top. Use a light box if needed. Keep the quilt top close to you so you're not bending over your quilt and you can stay relaxed. Back fatigue can set in if you are not comfortable.

Victorian Lace, detail, see the Gallery, page 76

The minute I saw this pieced quilt that my friend Mary Sue Suit had made for our joint quilt show competition project, I just knew the quilting had to be lace. Sometimes you just get lucky, and when this happens, you don't have to stew over what to do.

When I was trying to decide how to create lace, I found a stencil that I thought looked like it could be lace if it was connected with lots of lace-like connectors.

Stencil from StenSource International, Inc., by Barbara Chainey (www.stensource.com)

You can see in the following drawings how I incorporated this design over and over to give the lacey look that I was going for in this quilt.

There were a few things that I changed as I started quilting it because I was not getting the effect I wanted. You will know these things by just trusting your instincts.

THE FRAGILE WORLD, 80" x 80", made by the author

The quilting on this appliqué quilt was designed using the one-eighth design approach.

Inner design

After the design was enlarged and completed, I laid freezer paper over one quarter of the center. I folded it in half, designed the center, turned the freezer paper over, and traced the other half of the design. The center was marked with registration lines and divided into fourths. Then I was able to transfer the center design to the quilt with a blue water-soluble marker (Mark-B-Gone).

Designing a Wholecloth Quilt

One of my very favorite things to do is design and quilt a wholecloth quilt. I'm going to show you how to create a wholecloth design from your own quilting design by enlarging your pattern and transferring it to fabric, keeping it very square. Then you will be ready to quilt your wholecloth quilt by longarm, domestic sewing machine, or by hand.

A traditional wholecloth quilt will be very symmetrical and mirror-image in design. Think of balance and repetition to make your quilt more uniform in design. The main focus is the center motif; everything else should bring your eye to the center of the quilt. You'll have several surrounding borders that are complementary in size and design to the center design. Connect the borders so that each divides itself from the next border. You will be able to put different backfills in each area, which should be varied in size and shape to keep the quilt from being boring.

Wash, dry, and iron your fabric, although sometimes I don't wash my fabric because I like the extra texture created when I wash out the markings. The choice is yours.

Fold your fabric in half and in half again to make a quarter fold. Finger press the fabric as shown below.

Open the fabric to the right side. This is the smoothest side. If it takes you more than a minute to figure out which is the right side of the fabric, just go with either side. In many of the high quality fabrics it's really hard to find the "right" side. If using cotton sateen, which is one of my favorites, I always pick the shiny side.

Mark the center with a small dot or X with a blue water-soluble pen or chalk pen.

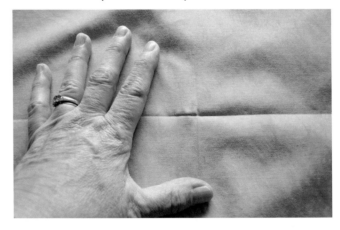

Lay a large square ruler on the fabric with the corner touching the center dot or X, making sure the square ruler is on the straight-of-grain of the fabric. Mark the square with a blue water-soluble pen. Some people will just fold in all the lines and use them for their registration lines, but I feel you get more accurate registration lines by drawing them in.

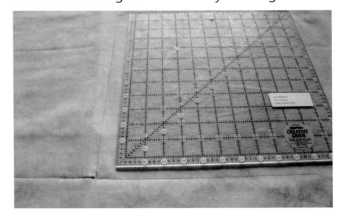

Using several rulers butted against each other, draw a horizontal and vertical line though the center.

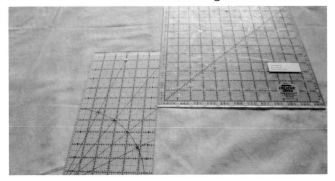

When I designed the pattern for HARP, I identified the areas that I felt needed improving. I cut out and moved some of the design, and other parts I cut out, corrected with a mirror-image design, and taped them back into the pattern.

Enlarge your wholecloth pattern using your preferred method. If you tile print the pattern, tape the sections together with regular tape, being very careful to keep the pattern straight and square.

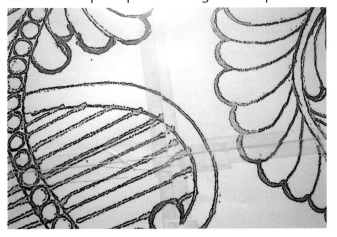

Tape the joins on the back with strong shipping tape and you will have a sturdy master pattern.

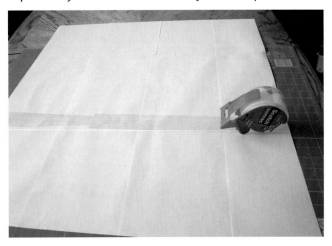

It is critical that your pattern be a perfect one-fourth of the overall design. Use every ruler you have to make sure it is square. Double-check this. If the design is not square there is no way you will be able to transfer this pattern to fabric and have it line up correctly.

Once the pattern is square and accurate, draw the registration lines on the fabric itself. I like to use several rulers to mark my outside edge. In the case below, the big square ruler is on the other side of the registration line. I used a 6" x 24" ruler and a 6" by 12" ruler. (Beware rulers that come with an extra half-inch on one side or end. They can throw off your whole design!) If you add the 24" and the 6" as shown below, the outside edge will be 30" from the center line. Mark the outside edge all around.

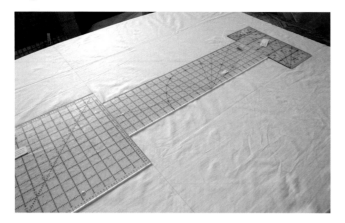

After outside edge and horizontal and vertical registration lines are marked, mark diagonal registration lines. These are especially important on a traditional wholecloth quilt to help position your quilting pattern.

Lay the 45-degree line of your big square on the horizontal registration line. Butt several rulers out to intersect the outside edge corner. Draw a diagonal line to the corner.

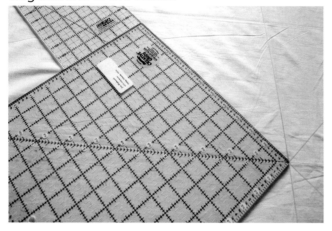

Place your registration-marked fabric exactly over the pattern, matching the registration lines. Pin in place so it does not move or shift and begin tracing your pattern with a blue water-soluble pen (my preferred favorite is Mark-B-Gone) or a chalk pencil (Fons & Porter) if you have dark or colored fabric. Don't transfer the crosshatching or

radiating lines. You will do this with the correct tools after your main pattern lines have been drawn on all four quarters of the quilt top.

Use your circle template to draw in the String of Pearls. They will be more accurate if drawn with the tool instead of by tracing.

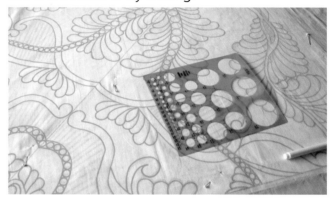

When the one-fourth pattern is done, unpin the pattern, move it to the next quarter, and transfer the pattern. Do this all around until the entire design is completely drawn.

You can now use your protractor and draw your radiating lines or use Renae Haddadin's Amazing Rays tools and draw your radiating lines (www.renaequilt.com). You are more accurate if you draw these lines on the top with the proper tools rather than if you trace them off your pattern.

Designing with Stencils

For those of you who are still a little afraid to draw your own original design, you can use stencils in an original way to make your own wholecloth quilt. Find a stencil you like and consider using just part of the design. Karen McTavish taught me how to do this.

Stencil SCL-404-16.5 The Stencil Co. (quiltingstencils.com)

I liked the fleur-de-lis in the corner, so I taped off the part of the design I didn't want to use with masking tape.

Using fabric that has registration marks, slide the stencil in so that it touches the edge of a registration line. Turn your stencil up and down and sideways until you find the best way to lay out the design with the stencils.

You can find other stencils with a "like" personality to form the next border. Slide the stencils in to touch the registration lines until you have your next border. Make sure you have breathing room between stencils, as a wholecloth needs lots of white background space.

I never try to think ahead of the stencil and border that I am working on because I don't want to limit what my next step in the next border should be. It starts taking on a life of its own as you build out your quilting design.

Here I started with a different center, using the parts of the stencil in a completely different combination than how it was originally designed.

Design developed using the stencil

Stencil SCL 018 04, The Stencil Co.

Designing a Contemporary Wholecloth

The process for designing a contemporary wholecloth is much the same as for a traditional wholecloth quilt. One of the main differences is the use of an asymmetrical design. See the next chapter for details.

WOODY'S GALAXY, detail, see the Gallery, page 72

Quilted Mariner's Compass

I think many quilters would love to quilt or piece a star or compass if they understood how to do it. I will take you, picture-by-picture, through this chapter so that if you follow me, step by step, you will understand it. Even someone who flunked geometry can do this. I promise.

Supplies

Compass
360-degree protractor
Ruler
Mechanical pencil
Eraser

Drafting a Six-Pointed Star

First let's draft a simple Six-pointed Star. Use a mechanical pencil for your early markings as you may be erasing some of the lines and circles later.

Extend your compass to its full length and draw a circle approximately 10" in diameter. We're just experimenting so the exact size isn't important.

There will be a tiny hole in the center. Mark it with a small X so you can see it. Use a fine mechanical pencil. In my pictures I used a heavy dark pencil so you could see the markings more clearly.

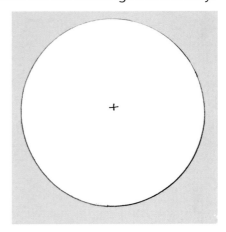

Lay your 360-degree protractor in the exact center of the circle. Mark every 60 degrees with a dot or small dash. Start at zero, and then place a mark at 60, 120, 180, 240, and 300.

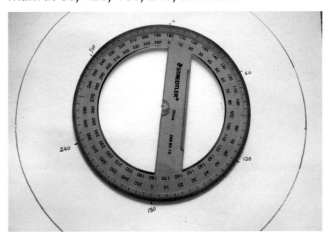

I drew the numbers so you could see where they are, but you will only need to draw a dot or dash.

Draw another small circle with the point of your compass placed in the exact center. Spread your compass out about 2" to form a circle 4" in diameter.

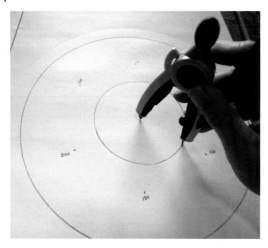

Draw a line from the center point of this circle, through the 60-degree dots you marked with your protractor, ending at the outside circle. If you place your mechanical pencil directly on the center dot and lay the ruler next to your pencil, and then move your ruler to line up with the degree dot, you'll be able to draw accurately through the dot to the outside line. Always place your pencil first, then place your ruler.

The first part of the registration lines for the primary star point is completed. Easy, isn't it?

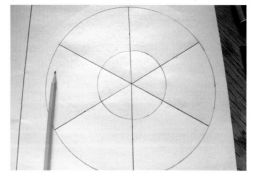

Draw a line from a registration point where the line intersects the smaller circle to the next line

that touches the outside circle. Now connect that outside point to the next line at the smaller circle.

Place your ruler at the center line of the star point you just drew and draw from that point to the outside circle of the next line. Do this all the way around until you have six star points. The six lines that we originally drew were your primary lines and they made your six primary star points.

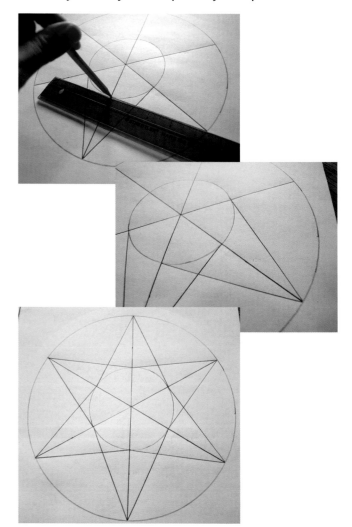

Now let's make our star more complex by drawing a secondary line to form star points in the middle of each of the star points you just drew.

Extend your compass to about 4" and draw another circle 8" in diameter, being careful to place the point on the same exact center of your Six-pointed Star.

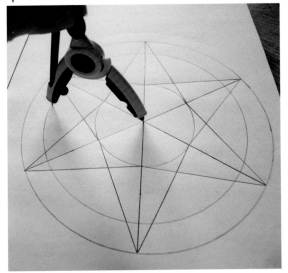

Get out your protractor again. Line it up carefully on the center X. Put the 0 on the original first line, which was at 0. Now we are going to put a dot (or small dash) on the following spots in your protractor: 30, 90, 150, 210, 270, and 330 degrees.

As you can see, these lines are in the exact center of where your two lines cross in the formation of your first star.

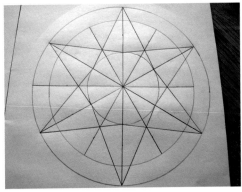

Draw all six secondary lines from the center point out to the full 8" circle as before, from where the primary line touches the smaller circle, to the new secondary line to the smaller circle. You will continue doing this all around until you have all the new star points.

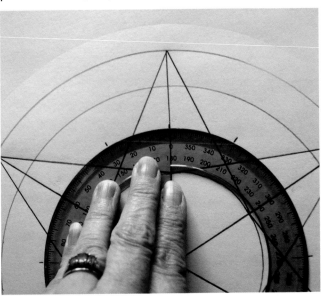

At this point you can erase any lines or circles you don't want.

If you have a smaller secondary circle (in this case, smaller than 8" but larger than 4") this will give you finer and slimmer points. A larger circle (greater than 8" but still less than the original 10" circle) will make the points wider and chunkier.

Play around with this until you get the size stars you want. The secondary star points may even extend beyond the original outside circle, making the secondary star points larger than the original star points. Or, it can be very small and just have little tips showing. You can have different size secondary circles so that every other secondary star is a different length. You can do anything once you understand the basics of the star/ compass design.

You can draft any size compass or star depending on how many times you divide the 360 degrees of the protractor. Traditionally a Mariner's Compass has 16 or 32 points.

Some commonly used star points are:
Five-pointed Star – mark every 72 degrees
Six-pointed Star – mark every 60 degrees
Eight-pointed Star – mark every 45 degrees
Nine-pointed Star- mark every 40 degrees
Ten-pointed Star – mark every 36 degrees
Twelve-pointed Star – mark every 30 degrees
Sixteen-pointed Star – mark every 22.5 degrees
Eighteen-pointed Star – mark every 20 degrees
Twenty-pointed Star – mark every 18 degrees

For the Five-pointed Star, if it's hard for you to figure out where the next spot is, just rotate your protractor around until zero is at the point you just marked and mark the next point at 72 degrees. Keep moving around until you have marked every 72-degree interval. It might be easier than

having to stop, divide, and find each spot in the protractor (72, 144, 216, 288, and 360).

Design Options

Woody's Galaxy, 30½" x 30", made by the author, see the Gallery, page 72

A contemporary quilt such as Woody's Galaxy started with an oval-shaped compass. After centering the horizontal and vertical registration lines, the star points were drawn the same way as explained above.

Put in the next protractor marks for the Twelve-pointed Star.

Try drawing an outside shape freehand.

Again, center the vertical and horizontal registration lines. Find a center and add your protractor marks.

Repeat the same steps for making the star points, only the points will be uneven. You can draw the inner circle with a protractor or freehand draw an uneven inner circle.

You can end up with some really fun stars that would be fun to piece, or just quilt as a design. You could even paint your star points, as my husband, Bill, did.

Once you learn the drafting method, you may want to add Flying Geese around your fun shapes or add partial stars in the corner as I did.

Now take a breath that you have probably been holding all this time. You can do this.

Marking for Asymmetrical Design

As explained before, fold your fabric in half and in half again to make a quarter fold and finger press the folds. Open the fabric to the right side.

Mark the center with a small dot or X with the blue water soluble pen or chalk pen.

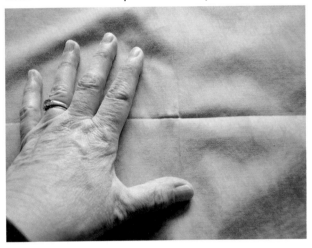

Use a large square ruler and lay it on the straight-of-grain with the corner touching the center dot or X. Mark the square with a blue water-soluble pen.

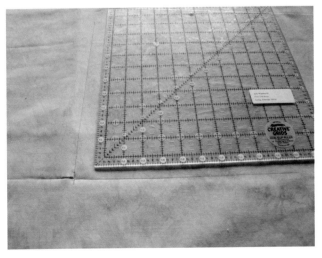

Use rulers butted against each other to draw horizontal and vertical registration lines.

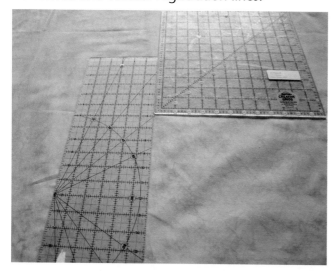

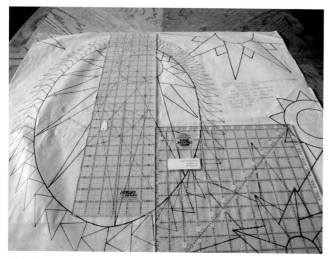

Also draw registration lines on your design.

Place your fabric over your pattern aligning the registration lines. Transfer the pattern onto the quilt top.

Quilting a Mariner's Compass

I quilted the oval Mariner's Compass design on yellowish-green fabric using pink thread so there would be some contrast.

WOODY'S GALAXY, front detail prior to painting

I used the same pink thread in the bobbin and pink backing. I wanted you to be able to see what using the same color of thread would look like.

WOODY'S GALAXY, back detail, see the Gallery, page 72

Patterns for Thread Painting

You can create wonderful patterns that you can thread paint on fabric. I like using black fabric because it makes the different colors of thread just pop.

Nature's Lace, 18" x 18", made by author, see the Gallery, page 77

I used three different pictures to come up with my rough drawing that I drew right on the black cotton sateen. I wanted to create a three-division composition with something up close, a middle area such as the ocean, and the farthest objects in the sky. This is a pattern-less, free-form kind of designing that's lots of fun and the end result is something totally unique to you.

I did this next quilt for a thread challenge in the Machine Quilter's Showcase competition of Fire and Ice. I took a picture of these Fire Roses with ice on their petals early in the morning. This photograph was my inspiration.

Sketch for my fire roses

Put the pattern under the black fabric and use a light box in order to see the design. I transferred the design with a marker called Chubby Chalk. This was before I found Fons & Porter's mechanical pencil, but the Chubby Crayon Fabric Marker did the job (see Resources, page 78).

Sandwich with two layers of 80/20 batting with scrim to give it the stability to hold all the layers of thread. Here it is, ready to quilt.

Select the colors of thread that you will be using. You need different values of your colors to create dimension in your design.

Pre-wind your bobbins. Sometimes you can get already pre-wound thread in the color of the top thread. My favorite thread is Glide by Fil-Tec. It has matching thread, already pre-wound. In this quilt I used A&E® Signature thread.

Your quilting machine, whether it is a regular home sewing machine or a longarm machine, can act like an embroidery machine. Quilt back and forth until you have the color and the

thickness that you desire. If you have ever used an embroidery machine, you will have noticed it sometimes builds up several layers of thread.

It is easier to stitch with one color everywhere it will be used, rather than switching threads to finish one area. Keep in mind where you want your light and dark values placed.

Stitch outlines of areas to be stitched, then go back in and build up the thread in between the lines. Your embroidery machine would do the same thing. This spreads out the stitching and keeps the fabric from puckering.

Start switching to the other colors and building the darker center of the leaves as you begin to build up the colors. Don't forget to look back at the darker center as you begin to build up the colors. Don't forget to look back at your photo to see where the sun was shining. You may need to use a pink thread with the red to give the impression of the outside petals.

Keep building up the thread to complete the thread painting. Remember to do all of one color at one time so you are not constantly changing your thread and bobbin.

Watch for areas that have not been quilted yet that start to form wrinkles. This is similar to making a child's smock and the stitching creates ripples of fabric just below the smocking. If you see that starting to happen, stitch some outlines in those areas to stabilize them until you can get to the heavy quilting.

If there is some distortion when you are done, spray the finished piece with water, block it flat, and let it dry.

Thread painting is so much fun. I hope you will try it on a small piece. Here is another pattern (page 48), inspired by an antique pin, that you can use for thread painting, (page 71) or to do a quilt in the stained-glass style.

ORIGINAL FISH, 17¾" x 24", stained-glass fish design, made by the author

When I did the thread painting I changed the design up a little. Once you like a design, try it in several different quilting techniques. This one could be pieced very nicely, too.

Patterns, Patterns, Patterns

I am going to show you what happens if you want to use something that is not a mirror-image design. It might be interesting to place my Roses design as a single unit in a half-square triangle in a pieced quilt. It may be better as a single design element, rather than as a combination of repeats in a symmetrical design.

Let's try repeating it. This drawing shows a grouping of the roses in a mirror-image, symmetrical arrangement.

Divine Rose pattern

It is okay. But maybe it could it be better.

I decided to make it into a radial composition where the design rotates around in a circle. It's as if the design is chasing itself around, facing the same direction. It is not symmetrical or mirror imaged.

Now you can see why, when you are first learning, you may just want to start with either a one-eighth drawing, or a quarter or half drawing before you decide on the repetition of the motifs.

Remember the fruit basket? It was my inspiration for this quilting pattern.

As you can see, I only needed to draw half the design. Its mirror image formed a beautiful basket in a horizontal composition.

I added a few lines to the stems that were my inspiration to give it more dimension.

Basket of Love quilting design

My daughter took a picture of an ornate decoration in New Orleans.

Photo by Becky Baird

This is my first little drawing based on her photo.

African Mask

I drew half of a design.

A mirror image makes one-quarter of the final design.

Putting four together, here is the final design.

You can see the final design is a long way from the original inspiration.

The caressing spirals I photographed at my daughter's house inspired my Feathers and Pearls design.

This is what inspired my Feathers and Pearls design.

I had Jessica Schick digitize this design. She also took elements out of the design for several secondary designs, which she digitized for my BERNINA embroidery machine.

When quilting a pattern, using elements of it along with the complete design will create a sense of unity. Most of the time it won't even be obvious that the patterns came from the master design.

I embroidered this pattern with my BERNINA and used blue thread on the orange fabric. These are complementary colors, opposite each other on the color wheel. They clearly show off the quilting design.

This pattern is just one part of my Feathers and Pearls pattern with a simplified design. Sometimes less is better. Again, I embroidered the pattern with purplish variegated threads. In my opinion, a design this complicated with considerable backtracking would have been better if I had used one color of thread.

Here's another example of taking just part of a quilting design and repeating it. I quilted it with my BERNINA embroidery machine and used matching green thread. This is what you would do if you don't really want the quilting to be very noticeable—more subtle and kind of hidden. In my opinion, I would recommend using a darker green thread, so that you can still see the design but it won't take over the quilt. Why go to all the trouble of quilting this if you can't see it?

I had such fortunate luck to have Sherry Rogers Harrison take my digitized Feathers and Pearls pattern (page 54), and turn it into a masterpiece, after she painted it and did the most incredible tiny, free-motion backfill. The first picture is a close-up of her quilt.

AUTUMN BUTTERNUT, 42" x 42", quilted and painted by Sherry Rogers Harrison, Normandy Park, Washington, see the Gallery, page 69

AUTUMN BUTTERNUT, detail

Drawing simplified even more

Look at the flowers I used for inspiration and see the pattern I designed.

The inspiration for Judy's Flower Garden

Half of Judy's Flower Garden

The complete Judy's Flower Garden design

The inspiration for Butterfly's Delight

Next let's look at this fence railing for inspiration. I really liked the loopy-sided heart with the curl at the bottom. It reminded me of butterfly wings.

This design was done with a ⅛ pattern.

One-eighth of the design

My photograph of the butterfly and flower (page 5) was also an inspiration for this design. To do this pattern, I printed out four of the one-eighth design, reversed to a mirror image in Photoshop, and printed four more. I left one copy uncut and cut out the remaining seven and glued them to the uncut page.

I could then scan it, enlarge it, and print the complete design. I think this would actually be a nice beginning to a wholecloth quilt.

The complete Butterfly's Delight design

Here's another design done from a one-eighth drawing.

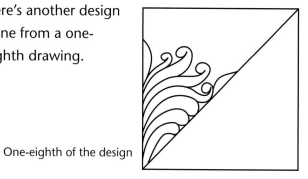

One-eighth of the design

The design mirror imaged to create one-fourth

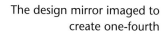

The complete Chrysanthemum design

This design was started with a half design on point.

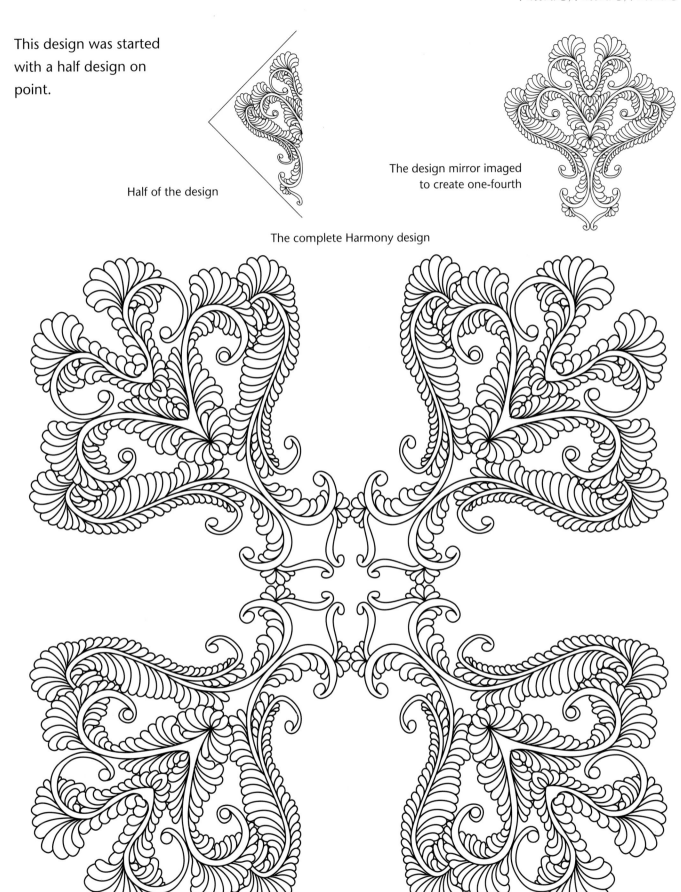

Half of the design

The design mirror imaged to create one-fourth

The complete Harmony design

Tulip design from page 16

Inspiration, page 24

Fins (design inspired by
photo, page 9)

Let's end with a free-motion design.

A Final Word

I have shown you how to take an inspiration and a single line or a curve and turn it into a stem. You learned how to make the pattern symmetrical and wonderful. It really is so much fun, and something you really can do.

Start doodling more and become more observant of the world around you. There are so many possibilities. Develop your creativity and I promise it will give you back such a sense of well-being. You might even finally believe you are an artist.

You can say "I am a fiber artist." And then don't forget to smile.

Thank you for sharing your time with me. Please send me pictures of your wonderful creations. jwquilts@yahoo.com
Happy quilting.

Gallery

AVATAR REVISITED, 67" x 67",
made by the author,
from the main collection
of The National Quilt Museum,
Paducah, Kentucky

HARP IN MINOR, 17" x 17", made by the author

AUTUMN BUTTERNUT, 42" x 42", quilted and painted by
Sherry Rogers Harrison, Normandy Park, Washington

Tumbling Rainbow, pieced by Carol Posthumus,
Rapid City, South Dakota, quilted by author,
pattern from *Big Book of Building Block Quilts* by
Sara Nephew, Hollow Cube

GOLDEN FISH, 12" x 18", thread painted design, made by the author

WOODY'S GALAXY, 30½" x 30", designed and quilted by the author, painted by Bill Woodworth with Stewart Gill® Pearlise™ paint (artistcellar.com)

HARP, 56" x 56", made by the author

KISS OF SPRING, 80" x 80", made by Mary Sue Suit, Sidney, Nebraska; quilted by the author

Here Kitty, Kitty, 77" x 52½", made by the author

VICTORIAN LACE, 82" x 82", original design by Mary Sue Suit, Sidney, Nebraska; quilted by the author

NATURE'S LACE, 18" x 18", made by the author

Resources

Adobe®
Adobe® Photoshop® family
www.adobe.com

American & Efird (A&E Thread)
www.amefird.com

Judy Allen
*The Art of Feather Quilting:
Golden Threads Series* (AQS,
2005)
www.goldenthreads.com

BERNINA USA
www.berninausa.com

Irena Bluhm
Quilts of a Different Color (AQS,
2008)
www.irenabluhmscreations.com

BOHIN FRANCE
www.bohin.fr/en/

Corel™
CorelDRAW™ Graphics Suite X6
www.corel.com

Digi Tech Designs
www.digitechpatterns.com

Dover Publications
store.doverpublications.com

The Electric Quilt Company
www.electricquilt.com

Fil-Tec Bobbin Central
Embroidery and Quilting
Solutions
www.bobbincentral.com

Fons & Porter
www.fons&porter.com

Renae Haddadin
*Amazing Ways to Use Circles &
Rays (AQS, 2010)*
www.renaequilts.com

Sherry Rogers Harrison
www.sewfarsewgood.org

Jan Krentz
Quilter's Design Mirrors
www.jankrentz.com

Karen McTavish
kmctavish@designerquilts.com

Pellon Batting
www.quiltlegacy.com

Roxanne International
Roxanne's Glue Baste-it
www.thatperfectstitch.com

Sharon Schamber
www.sharonschamber.com

Jessica Schick
Digi-Tech: Downloadable &
Printed Patterns for all types of
Quilting & Crafts
www.digitechpatterns.com

Anita Shackelford
Infinite Feathers and other
quilting templates
www.thimbleworks.com

The Stencil Co.
Cynthia Turnbow stencils
www.quiltingstencils.com

StenSource International, Inc.
Debby Bell
www.stensource.com

Mary Sue Suit
www.msquilt.com

Miracle Chalk
Chubby Crayon Fabric Marker
MiracleChalk.com

Ricky Tims
Ricky Tims' Rhapsody Quilts
www.thequiltshow.com
www.rickytims.com

About the Author

Photo by Bill Woodworth

Judy is an internationally known award-winning quilter, author, and professional machine quilter. Her first book, *Freemotion Quilting*, was published by the American Quilter's Society, and she has had articles published in numerous quilting publications.

Recently she appeared on *The Quilting School* with Linda Taylor and on *The Quilt Show* with Alex Anderson and Ricky Tims.

Her quilt, AVATAR REVISITED, won the American Professional Quilting Systems Longarm Workmanship Award at the AQS 2012 Paducah Quilt Show & Contest. The quilt is now part of the main collection of The National Quilt Museum.

Judy has been married for 45 years to her high-school sweetheart, Bill Woodworth. They have five grown children and ten grandchildren, several of whom Judy is teaching how to quilt. She is an enthusiastic dog owner and has three spoiled dogs.

Learn more about Judy at her website, www.judywoodworth.com.

More AQS Books

This is only a small selection of the books available from the American Quilter's Society. AQS books are known worldwide for timely topics, clear writing, beautiful color photos, and accurate illustrations and patterns. The following books are available from your local bookseller, quilt shop, or public library.

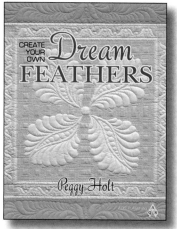

#8670 $26.95

#8238 $26.95

#8664 $19.95

#8532 $26.95

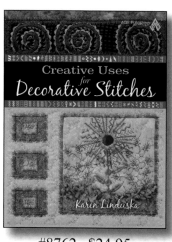

#8762 $24.95

#8671 $24.95

#8663 $24.95

#8763 $24.95

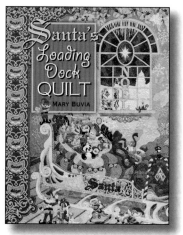

#8768 $26.95

LOOK for these books nationally.
CALL or VISIT our website at

1-800-626-5420
www.AmericanQuilter.com